The Work of a Winter

in memory of my father
and for my mother
and Malachi
with love

Contents

The Work of a Winter

Incunabula

i.m. Pat Boyle, 14 March 1930–9 May 2008

I

In my childhood home there was a room of books
left over from my father's days in Belfast.
They were toys to us. In hard-linen jackets
of primary reds and greens, they were building blocks
in the spare room, the one not needed yet for children,
its bare shell walls smelling thrillingly of plaster
and of possibility. Not a library, but piled haphazardly
on the floor, they were a magic mountain in our eyes.
It was my favourite place to play, to go in there at night
and 'write' – to scribble in their margins.
It was as if he no longer had need of them.
Those that made it onto shelves in later years
were paperbacks and full of optimism –
Carnegie's *How to Win Friends and Influence People,*
Teach Yourself to Swim, Teach Your Child to Read,
How to Lay a Lawn and then a big regal-looking book,
propped up and hidden in a velvet-lined box
that I was not supposed to find and that would
eventually be lost with all the others –
on how to make the perfect Catholic marriage.

II

My father made his first garden in that house
in Liggartown facing the Sperrins. He named it
Lynwood after a military march, my uncle's was *Belphegor*.
Tiny bricks came out of red metal moulds
like magic, like jellies. He riddled the soil for stones
like flour, the mixing of cement an alchemy of sand
and turpentine that made rainbow colours in the well
and chimed with the bubble in his spirit level.
He planted swathes of Siberian orange wallflower
perfumed for christenings and birthdays
that lived up to its name as the bee flower alive with sound.
Michaelmas Daisies were September flowers
and Livingstones fascinated when their pastel petals
went to bed at night, opening up to the sun like us each day.
Peppery lupins we anthropomorphised
into characters we visited on our bikes around the lawns –
the purple lupin was the teacher's house, the white,
the doctor's. Lilac and flowering currant were the smells
of my May altar and we had baby gardens of polyanthus –
the word seeming to grow in me as much as the flower.

III

He bought that house from a jilted Orangeman
who didn't know that land was not to be sold to Fenians
and tried to buy it back. Maggie Henderson
was Orange enough to make up for us – King Billy
looming in her hall and tea brewed for the 'wee soldiers'
who set up checkpoints on the road. Her quiet husband
Hughie walked with the Black Men in August. She kept
cats that reeked and snoozed on the roof of her henhouse.
They said there were dead Franciscans under us –
a medieval graveyard – but all we ever found were shards
of willow pattern when we tried to dig to China,
and the monastery overgrown at the turn of the river
where we went to play in the sheep tunnels under the
railway lines. The McCullaghs were our neighbours on the
other side who arrived bedraggled one night in a storm
when the electricity off. They came from the mountains –
'the Plum'. She had a countrywoman's disdain for pets
and drowned the only kitten I ever owned.
I would sing on my swing and imagine
that Paris lay beyond the hills.

IV

My father came to teach in Sion School when he was
nineteen-years-old, my mother in his P7 class.
He let her give out the pencils and directed her
as Buttons in the pantomime in the Bog Hall – telling her
at the dance that little girls like her should be in bed.
When she left school, she would wait for him at
Hamilton's Corner as he rode his bike from the town.
He wooed her with letters of his cricket injuries
and from a damp camping trip round Ireland
when his sister took him off to break it up and encourage
the bank clerk who had an interest in him instead.
They went to Belfast on the train to buy the rings
and were married by a priest who looked like
Montgomery Clift but who lost his mind in Biafra and had
to be carted away when he nailed himself and a woman
called Mary, who had the stigmata, into the parochial
house. They went to London for the honeymoon and
my father spent the flight talking to a hen man.
They poured the bottle of champagne left in their room
down the sink on the first night of their lives alone
together in the Frobisher Court Hotel.

V

We knew there was a ghost brother who had come
before us and who survived in our imaginations.
He became my sister's friend, included in all our games.
She held doors open for him, kept a seat at the table,
until his name was taken by a new baby.
The real child had been long-awaited,
only to die before he breathed.
My mother in the cottage hospital of the town
had no way to warn my father
and had to watch him walk the path of roses
to hear her lonely news. She – lying in a ward
with other women nursing – having been too tired,
a consultant annoyed at an interrupted game of golf,
an angry ward sister, a dead child.
He was taken away by her uncle in a Clark's shoebox.
She thought him buried outside the holy ground when
actually he was slipped into the edge of a family grave
that was blessed. It took years for her to tell of this and the
months that would pass in the high house that should
have held a baby – my aunt brutal in accusation
that walking to her mother's in the village was to blame.

VI

My friend Joanna and I would lie on top of haystacks
in Tommy Craig's field that sloped to the river
and try to work out how babies came. She swore
she'd seen her mother carry a bowl of blood
to the bathroom one night and that
must have something to do with it.
She was Protestant, so knew about these things,
and had parents who didn't go to church.
The Hoggs were Protestant too and had no children,
just a Pekinese called Suki. They would ask us in
to play Scrabble in a house full of plants, paintings
and books. Gwenda Lyttle told us that they sunbathed
in the nude. In summer the ghost beds of the flax dams
stank and the sickly smell of privet sent us to sleep.
On Fridays, we would go for messages to Strabane,
pour over magazines bought in the Bridge End
and marvel that the Osmonds lived in a place called Provo.
One night, after seeing a documentary on Vietnam,
I dreamed soldiers ran up Tommy Craig's field with guns.
My Granny told me that would never happen here.

VII

Summer started with the smell of a new book
bought in Bundoran in a huckster shop
full of wondrous things, like the stall of a relic seller
in a medieval market. We were staying in a big pink
pebble-dashed house in the West End where Mrs Brady
sang in pubs and the floors of the house were red
linoleum, the beds with iron steads high like boats floating
on a red sea. My book was Blyton and a cold wet July
in Ireland was dull compared to a leafy green English
seaside town. I vowed to have a midnight feast
and smuggled food from all our meals and hid it
under the iron bed so that by the feast's time
it was a feast of congealed rice and cold potato
– hardly lashings of ginger beer. And then
one night my mother bled a baby
with blood as vivid as the liverish floor.
I did not know it then but thought of it years later when,
at midnight Mass, a woman in the seat before us rose
and left just such a miraculous mess
on the gleaming oak of the church bench.

VIII

We would go to another country over the 'Camel's Hump',
the army asking us what was the purpose of our visit,
the white-shirted customs men taking so long
there was time to buy ice-cream cones in the queue.
That is where the milkman died
when he tried to climb the mountain,
my father would say, ritually, as we passed
through The Gap on the way to the sea.
And always, I saw the milkman in his uniform
scrambling over heather with six bottles in a holder,
losing his footing, the spilling milk become the frothy falls
we passed. Barnesmore was a Western pass
that might be closed by snow in winter
or where you might see Indians lining up on a ridge
ready to charge. I would pass the time singing pop songs
loud in the back – sometimes stumbling over lyrics that felt
risqué – *The Father, Son and the Holy Ghost,*
they caught the last train for the coast.
The Gap was our gateway into Donegal and safely through,
a new vigilance began – to be the first to see the sea.

IX

Rossnowlagh was a woman's place – the men coming
only on weekends with groceries ordered
from the payphone near the shop –
you couldn't buy the food in Donegal, where,
my mother said, they charged for turnips by the pound.
The caravan was cosy in the rain but we'd to chew
gum energetically to plug the condensation vents
around the windows, the gas mantles spluttering cosily
as the rain bounced off the tin roof and the waves
pounded in the background. On good evenings
the women and the wains set off on their own pilgrimage
across the beach and up the hill to the friary, passing
the big rock that marked the boundary of the lands
of the Four Masters and showed a gold-leafed monk
writing with a feather. The reward at the end – sweets
in Hursts' shop – the chocolate and crisps better
than at home. On some nights, all the children
would be rounded up for a midnight swim –
Mrs McCarron, a pied piper, luring us to the shore
with her Kerry Blue, the waves visible only
when the moon caught their white froth.

X

Summer ended in reverse ritual like a film rewound:
the last glimpse of the sea, chips eaten
in the car park of the chapel in Donegal Town –
my mother dividing up the fish and chips between us
so that wealth and adulthood came to be the dream
of having a whole bag all to yourself.
Then the journey through the Gap and the question.
Is that the mountain where the milkman fell, Daddy?
Then the customs post, the army checkpoint and our own
house grown strange and new from our long absence:
the garden seeded and ripe, the rooms impossibly large,
tans brighter in mirrors, piles of washing,
cotton sleeping bags that smelled of the beach
to be hibernated for the winter, left in the van
they'd dampen and mildew. The scroll of summer,
the back of an old roll of wallpaper on which I'd charted
ambitions for the long unformed open weeks of days,
could now be rolled up as time was parsed again
into the routine of days and hours and minutes
and we'd relearn the geography
of this older place – the house, the fields, the river.

THE DROLL YANKEE

The bird feeder arrives in an Indian summer,
its shiny Rhode Island patent promising
to lure woodpeckers, chickadees and titmice
with its silver tongues, its New England lore.

It will hang in our rowan and dispense
tasty American seeds to those who flock
to peck and pick and sit on the bendy branch
to chatter and shit amicably at their morning lavatorium.

How will our Belfast birds take to 'Yankee Trail Mix?'
Cracked corn and sunflower hearts bound in peanut butter
is food for visitors who do not migrate,
our birds more used to barmbrack and suet cake.

I remember my own shock the first time I saw
a cardinal bird stand on a Pennsylvanian lawn
stunning me with its vivid strangeness
like fireflies and strawberry butter.

The Puritans must have felt mocked
that garish popery had followed them across the sea.

And there was the maple syrup my pen pal sent
every year from the harvest of their trees in Buffalo, and it
would sit, gleaming and beautiful but untouched, in our
kitchen in Tyrone – we didn't know what to do with it.

The feeder works as though by magic
– silver hanging tower –
the birds fly into it in their old world forms.
Blue tits are busy buds on the bare tree,
our robin more russet than scarlet;
the coal tit our Mohican raiding party.

LATIN LESSON

I am studying Latin again,
the language lost in Loreto
where we learned the meaning of irony
choosing between it and history.

Our teacher was a young man,
puella puellae our first words
out of *Ecce Romani,* the verb
'to love' conjugated with feeling.

Pimply and pale, yet our young hearts
ran off with him when he
ran off leaving his wife,
our geography teacher, bereft.

Then it was a bent-backed crone
moving up and down the rows
in the dusty black robe that made her
a character in the world

we were reading of – something
strange, wizened, otherworldly, yet
she was gentle and led us into
the lives of Falvia and Cordelia.

And now I have come back,
but out the window I am watching
a wagtail dance in the neighbour's
slick new gutter.

He is a flash of yellow
and is dancing in the drain.

First I think he is the passerine
moticalla flava – the yellow moving tail

but then no, he is the more modest
moticalla cinerea and even
his yellow streak reflecting
the October sun-caught leaves

of a hornbeam and a birch, mean
that his name, there in the gutter
he has maybe taken for a rushing stream,
is derived from dust or ashes,

cinerea from which we get
the word incinerate.

Put Out the Light

i.m. Robert McCrea, 1907–1990

The entrails of a salmon flower in the sink
in the picture I have of you
teaching me to gut fish.

You have lifted it from the river
at the foot of our house,
the Mourne filled with Sperrin water

and now its insides stream
like river weed running in the current –
something of the river brought home.

You handle it tenderly, call it *she,*
a hen, and are saddened when you find the roe
that will not have a chance to spawn.

Another time, the weather in the window different,
you show me how to clean out a hen bird,
a turkey, that will hang in the cold till Christmas.

This lesson is serious, you say. *You must take out the lights,*
the lungs that hide in the dark of the turkey's vaulted belly.
Put out the lights and then put out the lights.

On ordinary days, you mush up Mother's Pride
to feed Rhode Island Reds, the smell of wet bread
filling the scullery for hens that scare my mother.

Those days, you had finished with the Mill
and the blizzard of the scutching room that gave you
Monday fever. How cruel that the weekend seemed to
mend you, only to begin again.

Proust's father gave it another name, *byssinosis,*
from the fine linen you were dying to produce
but would never wear.

At weekends, you would make a rosary of the village lanes
up High Seein, spitting into hedges with the other men,
knowing the name of every plant it landed on.

Winter Weddings

We are in the dark time of the year –
the world flipped over, fallen past the solstice,
but far from spring.
We must look for consolations;

the skein of geese that fly over Ballymacilroy,
the last crimson clusters of the crab apples,
the clean brightness of the beech bark,
the poolings of mist gentling the bare fields,
and the carolling of robins and blackbirds
in the holy evenings of the old year.

It is the fifth day of Christmas, St Thomas's Day,
who tells us *in the life of one man, never the same time returns,*
but we can follow the thread of time to another day
and preparations for another winter wedding.

The young priest is staying over in Number 14 Main Street
and an old aunt shushes him quiet, threatening to come
in herself. The trousseau of coffee and cream is ready –
the dress we will one day play dressing up with
and a bouquet of red carnations and fern.

Today, we tie the ends of time into a bow,
bind up the flowers of winter
and offer in them the beginnings
and the ends of love.

Ulster Haiku

Goldfinches, thistle-fed,
flash in the gloom of a wintry-spring
wearing the soul colours of the dead.

Botanic spring
the end-of-winter hellebore
pallid, pale, only just a flower.

Roseydandrums bloom
green-dark in early summer rain
around the still, dour house.

Invoking St Ciarán of Saigher

When the blackbirds begin to build their nest
against your house we take it as a good sign –
an omen of continuance, of the birds knowing it
a gentle place, trusting its rafters,
burrowing into the soft hydrangea,
coming right into the luctual house,
the house of the dead.
They swoop in – the rich open sough of their wings,
a sound bigger than themselves,
comic with beards of grass, busy with the build.
But at your Month's Mind, the birds are frantic through
  the night
and in the morning the perfect nest is overturned,
one small fledgling left by the sparrowhawk
upon the ground and the bewildered mother bird
still flying in with worms, unable to break her instinctive act.
I lift the scalding and feel again the cold of death
as I had on your cheek in the bright mornings of that May
  week
when I stole downstairs to be with you alone.
Now I wish I had the power of the Midlands' Saint,
whose prayer alone could bring back the birds,
could put the breath back into men when it had gone.

Stilled Lives

It is summer in the city
and here,
a shaded corner, come upon
while trying to find the Jewish quarter.

Life is lived behind these windows,
cameos of black stillness,
dark serene pools
opening onto the past.

Here are lives we glance upon
and glimpse
and leave again;
a bicycle in a hallway,
a book open on a window seat,
a bowl of redcurrants by a dripping tap.

What hands have clasped the latch of great wooden doors,
closed now on yellowing courtyards, sunny and silent,
weeds flowering in the cobbled cracks?
Old scholars shuffling to the library,
alchemists brewing gold in towers,
a wise woman marketing her herbs?

I love the crowdedness
of empty human spaces.

Mirabel-aux-Baronnies
after a painting by Pierre Bonnard

The afternoon wilts
as a thunderstorm looms.
It is siesta,
time to find
the well's dank darkness.

The room is like the flesh of a fig,
red and warm,
but the green of the trees
– lemon, gingko, oleander, bougainvillea –
stipples the walls,
washes the surfaces.

Cicadas sing – the engine of the trees –
honey-frogs and village bells
ring the distance of the hills.

Black cat lazy at her feet,
a girl sleeps in a blue chair,
dreaming deep into the earth.

The blue-glazed pot of zinnias
catches the light
and sends its scent over her,
as if it is always summer
and she is always there.

The Dutchman leaves an offering
of green beans by the window
and goes away.

The Sitting

after Conrad Faber's Katherina Knoblauch, *1532*

The first day he dressed me himself,
told me to wear Aunt Clara's necklace,
an enormous great thing, like a guild-chain
that weighs a ton and marks my breasts.

But I wanted to please him,
so I wore the cardinal-velvet from Heidelberg
and the gold girdle – I've had to let it out a bit,
I am swelling again – what will come, will come
in November, God-willing.

I like a winter child, lying in my feather bed
with the fire blazing, drinking honeyed milk
and cinnamon and Henry is good
about giving me my full time.

I don't mind sitting here in the courtyard,
it lets me see everything out of the corner of my eye.
We're under the medlars that I dreamt of
all through the last waiting.
Obsessed I was …
couldn't look at a medlar now!

In the spring, I'd go to his home.
I liked that – travelling to Aschaffenburg alone.
He lives in a street near the Bishop's Palace.
I'd slip into the back of the cathedral,
leave lilac in the Virgin's chapel
and light candles for my child –
then to the painting.

He bought me a song thrush to amuse me while he
worked and I'd plan the marketing I'd do before going
home, making lists of spices, candle wax and hemp.

He doesn't wash well.
He has that rank smell Henry would have if I let him
but he'd tell me how he'd mix the paint
and even let me taste the ochre once
when it seemed I needed to eat it.

The painting's nearly finished.
I will miss this sitting time –
little pools of quiet in my month
when I can go into my own space
as I am filled out in another.

The Rabbi and the Queen

On a sand bank by the Danube's neck
the rabbi sits and sways about his davening.
He has been left behind, bereft, wanting to go
to Eretz Israel. He has been left behind for temper.

On her way to see the Sultan, an Irish queen
is sunning herself before the harbour at Galatz.
She spots a creature moving back and forth – its long locks
tossing as if it is worrying its prey – she'll have it shot.

But one in her hunting party recognises Yossele
from the Polish town where he was emissary and returns
to plead the rabbi's case: he is a holy man and it will go
well for her with the Sultan if she takes him with her.

The Queen agrees – she can do with all the help she gets
– the seas being rough. But the rabbi turns away
and sniffs the air. He cannot travel on her boat
– she is unclean, a goy, a girl.

The queen hitches on a dingy and puts him there
but every night and every morning her sleep is thrummed
by his drone and she wants him. He is like a bulb.
She'd like to peel back the dark and silken layers.

She knows his skin will be like the snow-shock of the
monk she took to her bed the previous spring.
She wants to rock him under her like riding a dark wave.
But in all the voyage he will not even meet her eyes

and this arrogance is new to her. In Istanbul
she has the Sultan's favour. He provides
a vessel to take this Jew to Palestine, where,
she later learns, he dies at harvest time.

THE MAGDALENE READING

after Rogier van der Weyden's The Magdalen Reading, *circa 1438*

They have given me a book of hours
to read in chapel time.
I am not allowed to receive
– I have to be churched first.

They are afraid I will soil the book
as I have soiled myself,
so it is sheathed from my fingers,
in white muslin, like my hair.

My Latin is not strong
but I can make the sounds
and like to chase the animals
hiding in the letters.

It is not easy. I know what must be done
to hides to make this fit for holy words.
I have seen the flayed skins stinking in the heat
– the flesh peeled but little pieces still attracting flies.

Who will treat my soul with such care?
It will take years.

I know the brother who painted this.
It is pretty work. But I wash his stains
like all the others, pounding his sheets
so that my soul can be pure.

I have had to give away my rings and paints
but sometimes I steal his carmine,
or crush some cherries by the well
and smear my lips to feel myself again.

The Saint of Borromeo

The poor and the plagued fall from the doors of my city.
They come with the pain of loving and the stench
of loneliness in their mouths.
They scream and sing to me in the mornings and the night
and my halting words are no balm for their grief.

I came in the deadtime from the mountains
when even the berries were gone
and a gentle man touched me
and I knew that I lived by my laughter in his mouth.

They sit by the trees in the garden building fires with the
leaves – their hearts lie open in their chests
like red autumn roses – blown and frosted in pain
and I have no holiness that will warm those limbs.

I came from a place of empty eyes
where I could no longer see myself
I was not sure I had not died
for none would claim or own me.

They die in the halls of this palace
cold on the marble of its floors gnarled as the knotted
wood, spitting velvet blood and I must find the way
to consecrate their weeping crimson sores.

My people would bury me in a hole
and leave no trace of me
but this man loved me for a while
and sanctified my story with his time.

Disibodenberg

We climb the hill named for the Irish saint *Disibod*
the real meaning of the name lost in the long years
but these are the slopes he built his beehive huts upon
and *lived a bishop-abbot in the Irish way*
and set the scene perhaps for Jutta and her harshness.
In the rain among the dripping trees we hear
the story of Hildegard, come here a little girl
almost nine hundred years to the day.
I wonder at such a span of time
yet ... the cold and wet mixed with
the brightness of the autumn leaves and berries,
the smoking chimneys of the sleeping farms, the heron
our voices startle from his nest in the valley's stream
and the barking cranes that fly above our heads
– Brecht's metaphors of love – seeming lower and louder
than the skein of winter geese we'd see at home
but we are higher here – all seem to take us to that day
and the giving away of a child.

I've never seen an autumn vineyard before
and this morning the Rhine boiled and smoked with cold.
Was it like that the day her mother brought her up the
Nahe to hand her over? From the window of the train,
fruit trees grown in neat rows stood like shivering girls,
bare, their golden leaves pooled,
satin slips at their feet.

We make the ascent in silence – stopping only for
instalments of *The Life* as stations, me seeing what I can
understand of the German words mixed with the pattern
of the raindrops as a Dutchman speaks
under a red umbrella.

In the act of concentration, the leaves of all the trees
that brush my face are magnified and more defined

as though drawn by Hildegard in her herbals but
someone says she had her knowledge second-
hand, sent from God in her visions. I thought
such detail seemed to need the world.

There is more of the monastery left than I imagined
and glimpsing down into the walled space
that may have been the anchorage, its meaning
is clearer now – the anchor of the giant ship you see
in its shell, marooned upon a rock more stark
than when Hildegard came, the trees
that seem to speak of her, a Romantic affectation,
in her time a crag only, meadows and the primeval
forest far below in the valley instead.

Looking down into the walled spaces
that huddle at the feet of this place
Hildegard is one of the children
shown to Scrooge out of the folds
of the ghost's robe, a tiny child to act as weight
against all this stone and men.

On the way down the mountain we share
our stories, knowing it was light that brought
us here and vision: the one who sees
a woman gripped in sadness embraced
in the shadowing arms of a dead tree or the shoot
on the branch, the virgin bud that bursts
into a flowering Christ. One who can imagine
greening because she saw and smelled the spring.

Weather Vane

Your love, Lord reaches to heaven
your truth to the skies.
– Psalmody

I am on the roof this breezy day
in the sixth month of my pregnancy,
picking off the moss and lichen and tossing them
in soft bouquets to the ground.

Above me are the chimneys
– their stacks the colour of sand
and round the tops, circles of hearts
opening … to the sky.

I am a billowing blown crow
in my dark work clothes
and this is punishment for vanity.
For finding my face in a bucket of blue

Sister brought me up the back stairs.
The slates I clean are greens and shell-greys
that turn dark ink-blue in rain.
Today is a weather-breeder

the nuns say, presaging a storm,
so I am here to clean the way
and the rain will wash the loosened moss
in green runnels when it comes.

I am as high as the monkey puzzle,
Its open branches wide smiles
at the level of my eye, arms outstretched
– as if they'd catch me.

Down below is the road I will walk
my baby across to give him away
he, in a big dicky-up pram,
me, all dressed. Every Monday

the nuns take me to the parlour
to write a card telling everyone
who needs to know that I am well,
that the sea is wild, that I am working hard,

that I miss them, when all the while
I'm sitting at an oak table
– the smell of polish heavy in the air,
the grandmother clock ticking nearby,

dry spider plants on the windowsills
and a sad-eyed Mary hanging her head
in the corner. They take a lot of trouble
with the cards. The gardener runs them

up to Portrush and posts them there
so that the stamp's right, so that the postman
can tell everyone I'm grand
and it's not just my parents' word on it.

I talk to my baby up here.
We're not supposed to but the wind
takes the words away.
They say Our Lady had no pain

in either the making or getting of God
and she was allowed to keep him.
I'd have liked mine to have an angel for a father –
he'd have been light on me.

I mind my Granny saying
that when the midwife helping Mary
put her hand in to touch
it withered away.

Who'll help me when the time comes?
It'll be one of them and I think I'd love
to have that power to wither their hands.
My hands are cold; the first raindrops splashing

on the slate. The red bricks of the walls burn
in the dying sun's colour and the birds have gone,
taking the little offerings of moss and lichen.
They'll line their nests with them.

THE WINTER'S TALE

1

Emilia

I could not stanch her body that first night
when it seemed that every part of it was weeping.
She was sluiced all right and by no near neighbour.

I could not find her eyes – so lost were they in the flow of
face that seemed to melt as I looked into it
swollen in grief, animate, fluent with tears.

Her breasts wept too – azure veined and beautiful –
we padded them with cabbage leaves as the older women
said and bathed her in a bath of borrowed water.

This was no queen's chamber of her own where
white linen and flowers were readied for her welcome,
her withdrawal, her privacy, away from men.

This place was dark, piss-stinking – a heifer stall
where her calf came early and lusty
'from one prison to another', her mother said.

She would feed this child herself as if knowing
this was all she could impart before the severance.
It drank her in – the queen turned wet-nurse.

Where her daughter came she bled and we saved
the child's packing to bury under a winter thorn
where, Paulina said, something of this little one
would blossom from the dead.

When the child was gone she seemed to leave us too
delirious and dreaming, she was going out to give
the child a name and when we leaned in close to hear,
it was the name of the lost, 'Perdita', that came.

2

Hermione

The Winding Sheet

I dream I am lying dead in a yellow monastery
that sits on a hill against a sky blue as imperial sapphire.
The emperor of Russia was my father and this may be
Ipatiev he told me of – I can see the place where I am dead.

They are laying me out – the women
working in silence to the sound of vespers rising
from below in a stripped bare cell that is beautiful,
I can see this place where I am dead.

The cell is washed in the weak light of winter dusk
in the yellow monastery where the early sunset
blazes on the dome. My father was emperor of Russia
and I feel I have come home.

I am royal infant once again – naked and in care
of women's hands – my body never loved like this in life.
They work in rhythm with the chant – along my legs,
along my arms tenderly they tend me – I am not alarmed.

I am not afraid of death where I lie
in the silence of the yellow monastery,
these women love me and my winding sheet
smells of blue winter air and of rosemary.

The vigil of the night gives way to dawn.
With matins comes the sound of Russian bells.
Underneath the Mother-of-God icon
I can see the place where I am dead.

I am lying dead in the yellow monastery
on top of the blue-crowned hill.
The emperor of Russia was my father
in Ipatiev I lie cold and still.

3

Waking

I wake into the hardest winter I have known,
withdrawn into myself as to a cloister.
I watch the world from the widow's walk of Paulina's
home high above the town.

In this frozen time, in blue columns on windless days,
smoke from the small houses rises straight to heaven,
and I fly back down those chimneys to the hearths,
envying the women who can smell their children's heads.
I cannot remember how my children smelled.

On damp days the smoky stench of cinders rise
from the same fires and all is drenched and dripping
and I spend hours gazing and trying not to think –
my heart tuned to the tick of the clock in the darkened
room, my soul slowed to the thick time I must live through.

Sometimes I go out in disguise,
descend the hill from Paulina's house
and take the river way where everything is frozen.
Geese cross the winter sky and a lonely heron
keeps me company on the river.

She is marked in splendid greys,
her plumage always a surprise
against the drabness of the day.
Ahead of me the birds that haunt the temples of the dead,
goldfinches lace my way, flash like firelight in the gloom.

Where is my child?

I feel she has been taken from the earth,
banished in the blackness of her father's words
too dark for a little child to bear.
She is like one of those ill-born, misshapen,
a moon-child that slips away too soon
and is buried at the edge of things,
unmarked.

4

The Anchoress

It is fitting that he thinks that I have died
and we decide to leave things like this,
for in a way I have. Paulina will watch and manage
his slow, sweet penance and I will stay hidden,
like the woman of the Rhine I read about.

At Disibodenberg she wore a shroud,
lay prostrate on the chapel floor
and entered the blessed cell
to the sound of her own funeral antiphon
and the canticles of the dead.

But in that tomb she sees things with an inner eye –
visions of cities and heaven in the sky.
We will make of my life such a revolving door,
a *fenestra versatilis,* where sustenance and sacraments
can pass but I will stay unseen, immured.

5

The Quickening

At first I kept a winter garden which mocked me –
it was full of things changing form and dying:
the seeds of nasturtiums paled,
darkened and hardened into little skulls;
the heads of poppies were rattling noisy censers;
the ground a tracery of better seasons.

But then something in the year quickened.
After the equinox the healing witch-plant spidered
into bloom and bulbs crowning in the ground pushed
blushing crimson tips into a wintry gloom. The 'prickbush'
had its first leaves, purple and soft as a baby's fontanelle.
The hellebore, pale as a morning moon, drifted into flower.

As the soil warmed I could begin to finger it and find
the palimpsest of other gardens. I found
the eggs of things blanched by the dark like the seeds
of the apple of Carthage drained of their blood, and I
wondered what seeds my baby would eat underground,
that would seal her sentence and keep her away from me.

Venus is the goddess of small gardens but I am Ceres here
whose daughter has been swallowed up
where the earth opened under a blue narcissus.

This garden is my meditation,
and shadows tell the office of the day.
A robin comes and stands at my feet,
a blackbird is silhouetted against the sky,
his song in the pine tree choiring the hours
mixing with the voices of Paulina's girls at play.

6

Recovery

I am my own richness.

This ruched silk rustles.
It is the colour of pomegranate flesh
or of the broad bean flowers.
I glow and smoulder in it.

The sun burns upon this page.
I close my eyes under my hat
and let the noises of the day
drift over me;

pine cones falling into water,
the intimate buzzing of a bee,
the rhythmic beating of rugs from a balcony,
and everywhere – cicadas.

There is nothing more lovely
than the vista of a morning
long and languid and I am woman
storing up this day
against the coming bleakness
of the winter.

The Witch in the Wall

Fresh off the boat two women pick their way
up the slope of the town, their neat-shoed feet
in black-polished leather light upon and lean into
cowpats that give a little under their weight,
pleasantly oozing: the green crust staying firm,
the black ordure soft and threatening
to overflow – the force of things held momentarily
in perfect balance – as they struggle up the hill.

They are clad in black and their clothes
make movement slow. Their skirts of slub silk,
petticoats starched and underneath
liberty bodices laced, sprigged camisoles,
soft bustles upheld in a scaffolding of ribbon.
They are corseted, albeit loosely, and will be,
even in pregnancy, for decency. But that is in a future time.
Today they are on the road to Ballyvourney.

Their luggage follows them, equipment
for discovering the past. It is a pleasant summer's day
– the houses brightly-coloured against the sky,
gulls wheeling from sheer joy and the island is luminous.
They are here for the small figure honoured in the pattern-
day whose dust is said to cure sick cattle and banish
infertility in women – around whose well
an object would be passed from hand-to-hand
till outraged priests put a stop to that.

In the mid-years of the century these figures began
to be found – splayed where they would have been –
above the heads of monks as they trooped in for dinner,
straddling the lintels in churches,
perched on the quoins of castles.
It was first thought they were the Catholic Sacred Heart,
the chest walls held open for divine light to shine through

but then someone saw what it was hard to see, something
  else,
something they must be delicate in writing home about.

Not the walls of the heart then, but the secret place
of a woman opened on the world.
The women on the road to Ballyvourney
cannot conceive of a situation in which they would do this
  themselves,
hold open that part they have never looked at closely,
were taught to wash without seeing,
without disturbing too greatly.
They know its shape and texture from the other figures
they have examined in the Empire –
from Ptolemaic Egypt or from Ur.

Now suddenly they are shown into a farmyard
and its outhouses. There is the fetid smell of pig
from the stalls and swill and shit running at their feet.
This is a mistake surely – it is only a statue
they have asked to see. The local men, confused,
have brought them not to the place of patterns
but to a dark animal place wondering what business
such women could have with *her* – the pronoun personal
  and alive.

In the small room it is dark and they are dark in it.
It takes time to make out shapes. It takes time to find her.
By a low fire a woman is sitting and as they look
she hoists her skirt and turns to them – the white
of her thighs a shock in the dark.
She holds her skirts bunched, then thrusts her hands
into herself and opens her silent mouth – its lips big
and bulbous as a late and luscious rose.

The women are silent.
Stone is made flesh before them.

They must write this up, must report that in Ireland
at the end of the century it is not alone stone
that acts as an ignifuge, that plays its apotropaic part.
That near Queens Town, by St Gobnait's Well,
at Ballyvourney on the road from Macroom to Killarney
there are living hags whose bodies
are the dripstones of magic, whose intimate places
are as powerful as the Sacred Heart.

INDIAN STORIES

1

Darshan
(Hindi: the pleasure of looking)

In my favourite of your Indian stories
you are working in your room in the garden ashram:
the air is heavy with mangoes and dung,
the cows in the goshala sing, the saffron cloths
of the swami flap like prayer flags on the line.

You are working on the *Gita* intent and peaceful
but suddenly you look up and there is the cook,
Santakumar, with his extended family, smiling at your
door, and when you ask what you can do for them
he says, *no, no – just Darshan Mr Malki, just Darshan.*

And now, on many nights when you are asleep before me
I lie and look and think, *just Darshan, just Darshan Malachi.*

2

Mataji

You are by the Ganges at Bridge Ghat
on your way to the little teahouse
where every day a woman makes chapatti and dhal
on a low stove moulded from river mud.
She feeds you and smiles and you
have no words with which to thank her.

On this day the place is closed,
green, peeling shutters down
but you can see her through a gap, sitting,
surrounded by women who stroke her as she weeps.
Her hair runs in loose lanks over her eyes
and down her back – she is shrouded in it.

Her dusty husband is there to tell you cheerfully,
Mataji head-cracked – no problem!

and the next day all is restored.

How useful his tolerance now seems
that could allow
we all need days like these:
to pull the shutters down for stroking,
to close up shop and put the broken
head together once again.

Skitter

Ours is an autumn-coloured cat,
anorexic beneath her luxurious fur
mackerel-marked with a bindi
in the middle of her skull.

She has giant paws whose toes
are the alternating keys of a soft piano.
She is a pied cat really, a brindled one.
One foot blonde – the glamorous paw –
the other coal-black and sooty.
Sometimes shocked by its difference
she attacks it.

She follows us and the sun around the house
making herself a perfect circle in a pool of light
– unashamedly louche.
When it's dark she sunbathes under lamps
– beneath her fur – she's tan.

She watches birds from the window sill
making Hannibal Lecter noises with her teeth,
swinging her tale like a stripy pendulum.
But the birds are safe –
she has never learned to hunt.

Taken from her mother too soon,
she was found on a Falls Road skip with her siblings
by a milkman delivering to the convent.
Blind and mewling in the early-morning sun
– it's a trauma that haunts her to this day.

When we brought her home she couldn't bear her own
weight and we'd lose her in the pattern of the carpet.
All she eats alive are moths

who tickle her rough tongue
as she folds their flapping wings into her mouth
like a lady closing her fan.

She has a register of purrs
that change with her shape –
sometimes an owl
cruel and imperious
as the one who took Squirrel Nutkin's tail.
At other times a sphinx –
long on her haunches and regal.

When we travel we see her skinny cousins
scavenge under tables in the sun
and slip them surreptitious bits of fish from our plates
before they're shoed away by angry waiters.

Our Skitter doesn't know she's born.

Sheltering

It is the coldest night of the winter
the radio says
and I have been working late.
My study is book-padded, blood-warm
– the cold is double-glazed out.

Brushing my teeth I watch
wet flakes fall
behind the frosted glass
illuminated suddenly
by the security light in the yard.

I go to the middle level of the house
to look down
and try to catch in the act
the creature or shade that sets it alight
and that I never see.

But this night,
the coldest of the winter,
there *is* something there.

Right in under the grey guttering
a shape … a smooth white sphere,
is mimicking the whiteness of the snow.
The yard is all in darkness once again,
I do not know what it is.

I peer through the flakes,
aware of the cat snoozing by my feet,
and then I make sense of it.

Perched on some ancient pipe tie –
the full moon of its belly brightened
by the black of an eclipsing breast –

a magpie,
is sheltering
from the snow for the night,
its head tucked in
and only some small
feathers fluffed out in the wind.

I climb up to bed, snuggle in to your warm back
and fall asleep, content in knowing not how but that
this old house and we are somehow blessed
for sheltering an extra soul tonight.

Christmas Box

There is honey and chocolate on our doorstep
since Christmas – sweet box and coral flower –
one on either side. The heuchera with ruffled
cocoa-coloured leaves hunkers in the corner but
the sarcococca or sweet box is where we step
inside by design so that on nights as dark as winter
and full of storm we brush the bluff, squat, shrub
and boots and coats trail the scent of summer
into the hall. Its flowers are what are left of flowers,
petals blown away – spindly threads ghostly in the leaves,
the odd, early blood-berry that follows.
Its genus *confusa* is right – from so frail a bloom
a scent so big, as if the bees have nested in it
and are eager for their flight.

Louvain

i.m. Kate Alexander, 1926–2007

I know you are not
the pink-throated bird that flies from the ash
and hovers at the window before disappearing in the dark
May dusk.

I know you are not
the blackbird singing in the Belgian square
as the tour guide speaks of Janssen, reading St Augustine
in his tower.

I know you are not
the tulip tree in bloom in the Botanical Garden
slender and splendid, the flowers red-veined but green

or the liquid amber tree
or the silver back hens that remind me of your Silkies –
on this my first journey that I will not be able to turn into
story for you.

I know you are not
in the tranquil place of the Beguinages.
It would have suited you, a city of women before or after
men and not quite nuns!

I know you are not
the slender beautiful girl who climbed the Buddhist
mountain – of whom you'd have been so proud tracing her
lineage for me to your home place.

I know you are not
at your table in the corner of the warm kitchen –
searching among papers – your long fingers making
important each thing you touch.

I know you are not
in your garden, tending the little yellow lilies that host
the door so briefly and do so now unremarked by you.

I know you are not
the presence I think I feel in the old house
getting up in the night, not here in the turn of this season.

Black Mountain Viewed from English 6

Sometimes in the middle of a class we'll stop
and look out the window. It is the highest and
biggest in the school and framed by it is a sweep
of mountain that gives a sense of the west
of the city. The little streets become beautiful
geometry as the light catches identical parades
of chimneys grey below the mountain's green
and on the top a lazy orthographic cloud
will lie along it in the morning until moved
or melted by the sun. And one day there's a fire
with the fireman up a ladder peeing his water
on a burning house and every so often a sun-burst
of white gulls will wheel upward lifting like a surprise
across the rooftops and the tall row of poplar trees
that bind the nuns' graveyard have been pollarded
stark against the winter sky and often weather
will roll in and down, rain bleaching all the colour
out to a grey blur, only for it to come back
in bright contrasts after the shower.

Amelia

Amelia is believed to be the ghost who haunts The Crown Bar in Belfast – a prostitute who died after being thrown down the stairs of the brothel above The Crown in the 19th century. The adjoining street is named for her.

Come into me, come into me,
for that is what you've always done:
men of Belfast gather under my dark skirts,
seek shelter in me out of the rain, taste me
when the taste of their own lives is too bland
and needs savouring. I gathered this city
under my dark skirts and all its stories are in me now.
Belfast was *her* city – Victoria's –
but this was its Crown and I one of its jewels.

We were all painted flowers in this darkened glasshouse
and I the gardener of lust – that forced, black, sweet flower
that flourishes where greatcoats sizzle after rain.
I could make any puny plant grow with the touch
of my hands, swell the stem into life
till the sap rose to the tip. In here
there are blooms everywhere if you look:
roses, apple-blossom, lily-of-the valley, fleur-de-lis …
bridal flowers and we would make

a kind of union in the snugs. Toffs would take me
up the stairs to the rooms but the poorer
or the meaner men, some little commercial traveller
in his shiny suit just off the train, would want to play
the gentry in the snug, guarded by gryphons,
sitting up on black leather he'd want
to ring the bell for service, the bell
that would set fluttering its gaudy striped pennant
like rare collected petals under glass.

In those days, I was always in the gaze of men.
The first wrong thing I did for a man …

We were the only women in this place
except for the Sally Lassies who would come in
in their black bonnets to save us and then
the women in the mirrors holding sheaves
of hops and maize and the wee Cupid wains
over the bar. I am now the one who hides
in mirrors. I am now the gaze.

The men would bring the excitement of the streets
in with them – the royal visit and the big ship.
One man had seen its launch and told of its great
dark bulk and how they used a ton of grease,
motor oil and tallow to smooth its way,
to lubricate it on the slip-way like a great whale
and ease it down and in and in and down and then
it began to slide, to go faster and faster
and faster until at last in a giant gush

it settled upright on the water. They cried
after it went down – the news wailed by a boy
on the corner in a cold spring evening but I thought
there are worse things than letting go … living forever
may be one. The men of various wars have walked
the street of my name seeking solace in its Angel Paving
and in the years of the last troubles
men would once more use the snugs like beds,
only this time because

they could not go home and were afraid.
Sometimes I thought the sounds
would blast me out of here on a devil's wind
but the dust would always settle. Now
I have new things to see – especially the women
who take the space and the men

on their own terms so I may stay a while longer
for there are more stories to hear and in new tongues,
more flowers of lust to water and to tend.

The Visit of the Wren
Annaghmakerrig, October 2011

On a dripping day that never really wakens
when the sun is weak behind the line of Gothic firs,
flaring through the clouds sometimes like the flames
from a distant winter war, my head is in Fallada's Berlin
and there are lights needed for reading in the afternoon,
the old glass of my window becomes a focus for the birds.

There are blackbirds landing in a lichened birch –
the branch giving under them to hand them
delicately to a lower ledge like a dancer
passing on a lift, then coming down to the ground
to scuffle, tail up, in the gravel and the wet leaves.

Suddenly from a lamppost a spray of little passerines
flow like a wave from tree to tree – from the ash
with its ghostly white berries and the spindly birch –
wenny and mouldy with lichen. A giant Irish jay
prances on the lawn – too big and colourful to be real –
like one of Hoffman's mechanical toys he'll make a lesson
from.

I have been a happy hermit here
and when the wren visits the windowsill a great tit
hangs on the stone and stares in; a chaffinch,
lemon-grey and then the rosey male dip their heads
into the coppery gutters that splutter with rain.
The old house is lit from the outside in.

JACINTA PAINTING UNDER TREES

for Jacinta O'Reilly, Annaghmakerrig, 2015

Jacinta is painting under trees
capturing every note of the birds' song
on a canvas that is netting the spring air.
From here, she is a child or a 1950s mother
hauling out a quilt to dry on the clothes' line
something deemed unseemly now for gardens.
My mother saw a full line of bright white nappies
flapping in the wind, the pristine fruit of her morning.
Jacinta hangs her work from the trees on Easter branches
buds ready to burst, daffodil smears of yellow in the grass,
a blackbird scuffling among the dead leaves of the beech hedge.

Jacinta leaves the painting out on the grass overnight and
tends it with a blue bucket in the morning. Is she adding to
it or plucking off what it has snared? The stray feathers of
a crow or a bee that has trespassed in the paint? Perhaps
the coarse hair of a puzzled creature that sniffed it and
this minute carries off the colour to its lair? When
this painting hangs, will it hold the outside in?
Does it know it is *en plein air*? I have never
seen a painter work like this and envy her
the chance to play which is surely what
art is. Jacinta is painting under trees.

The Photographer of the Sky

Once then, the pull of the day
being just too strong, I walked out
into the mouth of the day
– wide, blue, indolent –

stunned by the light
and brightness
of a September afternoon.
Staggering from the matinee

I left the Kawabata child poised
and squinting in the studio space.
I cannot look at eyes any more
I am tired of faces.

In the weeks before, I would
pan   wide   of   them
zoom to the backdrop of clouds
and rest there

creating people-less portraits
of a world turned upside down
– revisited from days of summer childhood
when hours lying in the sun

would make the sky-world
the real place, this one
transitory. Once more
I needed to foreground the sky.

That first day I crossed the city
by its parks where gardeners
were tamping the ground in cleared beds
ready for planting.

Above them the yellow gingkoes
captured the light in their winged leaves
and canopied the workers
drinking in the tea houses below.

I was outside of my place, my rhythm,
like a child whose illness is a pass
to the mystery of his mother's day
but I wasn't going back.

I came to a hill station above the city,
where I would hike with my father
on days when the radio announced,
the arrival of the cherry blossom there.

He would bribe me with sweets
and tell me tales of long ago when
'the quality' would come to make ceremonies
of the first viewings of the flowers and snow.

This is a good place for me among the pines,
a hide, a dry, black box to frame the forest
and the sky. My pictures now taken in my mind,
the lens my retina, the shutter-speed the closing of my eye.

I am not entirely alone. In the grey dawn
I hear the temple bell – monks dropping
a pebble of sound into the well of valley between us,
dark blooms among the cryptomeria.

I begin work early, wakened by the cold,
focusing on the thin line of crimson in the east
that is first a map line, a boundary, then a vein
that bleeds its colour slowly through the rest.

In the early days the sky is often blank
and I put the cinnamon bark of rhododendron,
the persimmon or the plum-red pollen cones
of the bodkin tree against it, for contrast.

And before the thunder and snow-holding clouds,
one night there is a yellow harvest moon
so huge it lights the forest like a stage
and shows me theatre in the trees

– white masks lucent in the dark
like lacquered bowls of the shadow world
that needed candlelight to be seen.
I am now an audience. I find beneath the pines

the neat possessions of their lives
in little carefully-attended piles,
sheet music, shopping lists, a violin,
the small badge of the salary man

pinned to a lapel; the work of my own craft
that caught in different moods the connections
they have now chosen to sever – lovers, mothers,
children all discarded at the feet of trees.

And when the clouds do come and I explore
their mountains and their seas – it is these I will see
who could not hold their visible shapes any more
than I and fled to the welkin world instead.

LILACS FROM THE FIELD OF MARS

Bringing armfuls of lilacs from the Field of Mars
blushing girls hide them under cotton skirts,
stiffening petticoats like the dancers' horsehair net
bought by the shimmering bolt they have seen carried
to the costumier's in the neighbouring street. Once in place
they must brave the babushkas who sit in the dusky
corridors of the old theatre knitting, darning the dancers'
shoes, holding the block in the satin where blood has
soaked into cloth. The hidden flowers rustle as they walk
and when inside are pulled out in a wash of spring scent
to be handed carefully over the balcony and down to the
blind box where they will wait until the last beat of his
pas-de-deux and then fall in a lilac shower. Flowers warmed
by the thighs of girls as offerings for the young god.

Nureyev

When people listen to Bach they hear God, when they see me dance I am God.
– Rudolf Nureyev

1

Born on a train, his first breath pulled
out of the depths of the ancient lake where Christ
came and declared that beyond it there was nothing.
Born with the smell of ice coming off its sweeps
too early for spring, some old spirit of the deep
entered him, the fluidity of a fish come into his spine,
blown on the Barguzin that first night and day,
sunshine found him and a restless soul.

2

In the photograph he carries with him he is a small child
sitting on his own knee – the grown one in drag as if to
dance the nurse in some forgotten ballet. He is beautiful
and sun-tanned from the fields in printed summer cottons
without the scar on his upper lip – his mother's face
that he would forget if it was not his own.

In the heady years, he will sometimes find a time
to phone and be transported to their small room.
He can conjure then the smell of a Russian summer
or the sour sweat of his father's work clothes
and his sweet tobacco. He wonders if his father was still
a dreaming boy, kneeling to pray in the madrassa,
would he take his call and speak to him
without anger across the acres of time.

When he visits his mother once in the new times
she is in an empty room with only an oil lamp
and an old kilim and he thinks of those
he collects in his Paris apartment
and wishes he could show all this to her
that would seem the wealth of a Czar.

3

When Avedon asks him to dance and captures him,
he stays at the end of the shoot to ask
if he would be photographed dancing naked.
He has done this once before as a boy, danced
unhindered by his clothes, feeling divine in a field
where the corn shielded him and where each step
left a trampled damage. He sees a look in the
photographer's eyes that will become a look he knows.
He says yes.

4

He flies over the Canadian wilderness to the hospital
where Erik is dying. Each has tried to be the other's life
and it has not worked. Entering the room he remembers
Erik's story of once, as a little boy in Denmark, going out
of himself as he sat ensconced in an apple tree, heard
his mother's call for dinner and saw himself,
a little boy sitting in an apple tree, his mother calling.

Now he must climb up onto the surgical bed
as if they are both children, as if this was their first
ever dance, the holds to be worked out so carefully
since held wrongly he will fall. Now it is a case
of finding places to hold, to move their limbs
among the tubes and in ways that will not hurt him.
Now there is no more movement, only the hold.

Rudik, who was so rough with him in their lovemaking,
is now the gentle one, now the one
who holds him from behind realising how light
he would be to carry and there are no more words.

He will hear of the death on his island.
Sitting on a balcony with a friend,
bathed in the smell of night jasmine
he will say 'Erik died today'.

SETTING OUT

i.m. Seamus Heaney, 30 August 2013

That morning our house was at its most alive
full of the busyness of the end of summer
the windows lit by the pinks and reds of flowers
at their most vivid in that Lammas light
deepest just before they fall.
We would have spoken of you
with the painter come to paint the shelter
for the winter logs – himself the brother of a poet.
And then into the light and laughter
– the phone call and the news.

Later on, I'd picture you a kind of Tollund man
spiriting yourself up and out across the bog,
storing your bundle of soul-clothes,
as you'd seen the turf cutters do with your father
but this time having no fear of the plashy wet,
the tell-tale places of purple water mint.
Lightened and buoyed across the causey
through a meadow of bog cotton/asphodels
you go with long clean strides to meet your father
and hold him properly this time.

THRUSHES IN THE ROWAN TREE

The very day the rowanberries ripen, thrushes fly in,
stately and speckled, as if summoned there.
They turn the tree to illustration, an autumn square
in an illuminated script, or a sultan's tree of singing birds.
Acrobats in motley, they swing, making lithe lines
of branches, stretching – somersaulting out to reach
the berries – each red drop held in the beak before
it falls to add to the marble bags of their bellies.

And, just as quickly, by timing only they can tell,
they leave at once to their own applause
to come again and work their stripping circus act
one level at a time, methodical, exact,
until the tree is bare and they have left
another square: a silhouette of winter.

The Work of a Winter

St Antony's, Leuven, 1643

1

It is September in the garden,
the time when I would always turn for home,
when all roads would lead me back to Donegal,
to the valley of the Eske, to the mountains of my first
name, to that great cove of my father's place
and the little village by the Drowes,
where a makeshift scriptorium under eaves,
had been readied for the work of a winter.

I'd been travelling all summer on the roads,
browned to the colour of my robes, like the men
we'd pass at harvest, who'd toss a word and wave
at us and sometimes bid us share a chunk of bread.
We were harvesting too but this harvest was from the old
black books, dark as the soil, my job to transplant stories
onto clean, white ground. It was work I'd been reared for
as much as those men for the fields.

By this time of year all signs would point in that one
direction – the bramble leaves already blazing in the
hedges would be beacons lighting us home, blackberries
forming out of blossom make a trail, and swallows
swooping in the air before us were heralds announcing
our return. And sometimes in the winter
I'd find myself walking in my dreams, always walking,
still following the long ribbon of the road.

2

The garden here is formal: there are pear trees espaliered
on the wall and green and golden pears stick out
at all angles. Until recent days I would still help
to pick them but now I am allowed to rest
– to be an 'omelette dreamer' – as the Spanish say
of old men here. We are in the square of the Pig Market,
this house once the House of Blackbirds who have never
left us, singing us to sleep on summer evenings.

Those nights I would often long for home,
for the white nights of Donegal and for Kilbarron,
when the sky beyond the mountains would never go
completely dark and I would sleep to the rhythm
of the sea and wake to the smell of oats
bubbling in the porridge pot and the glimpse
of chimney-sky as I helped my mother, Honora Ultach,
check for birds before the lighting of the morning fires.

We were a perching house, set at the very edge of things,
the castle walls contiguous with the cliff,
precipitous, seeming set one day to tumble
into the waves below. It was never silent
since the sea was always speaking: shushing
us on quiet nights, thundering in storm, sending spumes
of white waves nipping at the castle's ankles like terriers
and sometimes showering us with foam.

3

One of my brothers is burning leaves down
near the willow tree where I have asked to be laid.
The blue smoke hangs in the still air of Leuven
and makes it sweet and sleepy. I'll be happy
to rest here in this flat land where the horizon
is always lost and faraway, not like the big skies
of home when you'd think sometimes
you could break the veil and see right into Heaven.

From our high, windy eerie I'd look across the bay
at mountains I climbed as soon as I was able
– great, rounded rocks with lakes on top that I thought
still held the waters of the Flood. They were best
in this soft light of Lammas time and I'd sleep up
there under enormous skies and they called me
'Tadhg an tSléibhe', 'Tadhg of the Mountains'
– since they were my second home.

I knew the brown-robed men from when
I'd seen then walk the strand in prayer,
their rough robes blowing out behind them
billowing in the wind or sometimes running
out of the sea like boys, their tackle swinging
like a fresh-caught catch. And then more sober times,
before the fire, when my lessons began and I'd to learn
the *seanchas* – the lore of place, of poetry, of men.

4

I ran away from the road that was laid for me
for a long time and came here first a soldier,
not a scholar, riding horse in the Irish regiment
of Spanish Flanders. Those were good years too –
I loved the horse and would miss forever the feeling
of its life below me when I took St Francis's Rule
in all humility to stay lower than it always
and never ask it bear my weight again.

But even in those years with worldly men and their
women, I was really God's – keeping the childhood faith
of making every minute of the day a remembrance
– so that when I woke to put on clothes, each part
would take me to the Passion of the Lord:
closing my buttons meant the scourge, putting on
my shoes the nails and going back to bed with the night
would remind me of the tomb.
The day was punctuated in prayer.

And when I did give in and came in here,
it was too late for the Latin, so I would use
the wooden key to Heaven instead – the Irish tongue of my
place. I'd do the chores like all the others in the warm
kitchen, in the garden here, but always headed for the
page. I'm no poet. I was not to make a new way –
only to follow the old books' paths. My job when it began
was questing, but questing stories instead of alms.

5

Strange how the prayers of your first life become
the prayers of its ending: I word my mother's prayers
on these beads made from the seeds of peonies, from
the garden of the great Abbey of Donegal.
All the sweetness of that lost time is the blown rose
made small but it opens for me again in memory: visits
to the Abbey before its sacking, on the Feast Days
when it was a place of gardens and orchards
and continual chant.

The Abbey was a home from home, open to the sea
and so near the mouth of the bay that the boats
would sail right up under the windows of the refectory,
so that the coarse talk of the sailors would drift up
like smoke through the different music of the *Lectio Divina*.
In the paper markets in Antwerp I would be back in that
busy Donegal, all open windows and talk, all colour come
from far away, the bright day blowsy with excitement.

When I returned, we were in refuge from the Abbey
and all the grandeur gone. We called it our wilderness
place, *in deserto nostrae mansionis* – a humble river mouth
fed by the waters of Lough Melvin and the sloping hills –
no gardens or gold, no orchards in the rushy land.
We were lying low so as not to draw the world
to us or our busy hibernation, like the Seven Sleepers
we hoped we might wake one day to a world transformed.

6

I remember my first journey out of Donegal.
I'd started with a cousin's book – which had
The Law of Adhamhnáin who'd decreed
that women should service neither soldiers nor their wars
but then laid down the law on what they owed him for this
favour. I took his vision later from the book of the Dun
Cow and prepared to send some leaves here to let them see
the work, but there were hard parts in it that I needed
a scholar's eye on first.

At Lughnasa we made Dublin. The *Rule* forbade me
go alone, my socius on that first journey a gentle man
from Legfordrum who talked about his father's home.
Dublin was poor pickings because the libraries and our
houses were suppressed – the vellums sacked and
banished and even with the use of the heretic bishop's
books we found only the rule of Columcille
and a poem attributed to Brigit.

Then the *Scúap Chrábaid* – the Broom of Devotion –
that always reminds me of Kilbarron and the bisom
made of reeds that my mother or the maids
would sweep round the house, shooing me out of the road.
This was a broom to brush up evil and in copying
its invocations of the far world and of Heaven,
I felt I was sewing up a cloak of prayer and of protection
that I'd take with me, a breastplate for the road.

7

Working on the old books was like swimming in a bog
hole – it would leave you dark and smeared, as speckled
as the *Leabhar Breac* and weary; pages spotted
with the imprint of a mouse's foot or the holes of a worm,
marred by crude mendings but then surprises too;
the unexpected outline of a flower, a crucifixion,
a horse's back the spine of a letter F, as if lying in a sweet
meadow kicking up its feet in the air in freedom.

Sometimes the vellums were so brittle you'd be afraid
they'd wither in your hand and disappear. Other times
they'd be damp, defaced or smell of mould, especially
if taken out of hiding. I'd copy first in summer
then retranscribe at Drowes. It was never my job
to comment on or change, even when the old words
offended sense or meaning – mine only
to transpose onto different ground.

We whitewashed walls to save the light, the page
become a bare white field ploughed for winter sowing,
my words a blackbird's track on snow or the spiky
branches of a hawthorn hedge, the letters black and spare,
in simple single lines. We did away with columns,
left space around each entry, liking what a rabbi showed
me once; their holy book left ever open to addition
in another hand and in another time.

8

The brother has gone in and left the fire and a woman's
voice from the Begijnhof wafts in with the blue smoke
of leaves, gentle as the midnight singing in the dark
of the Clares of Lough Ree. I went there near the end
to copy the book of their rule, a workaday one
for the hard life they live, day in day out –
I felt guilty to be setting down their austerity so starkly
and I cannot say I was not glad to leave them.

It's a sore existence they have there in the wet heart
of Ireland. They all take a part in the drawing of turf
and water for the house, tending a mucky garden
in the rain in neither shoes, nor socks, nor stockings.
They wear rough wool against their skin
like the robes of St Clare, who thought
the homespun velvet and the rope a jewelled belt,
her wooden slippers gleaming gold in the tiny light
of Mary's altar.

They say she loved the rain on the hills of Spoleto
because it was a link to Francis but rain was rare in
Tuscany – we had no such problem, there was always rain.
They prayed so hard and so unceasingly
that midday seemed like midnight and even then
they'd be up and at the matins. I stayed two days
and they are praying for me now and will be at my death.
That was their promise for the book.

9

Lough Ree was the closing of a circle, for there
we'd worked as four for the first time: the two Cú
Choigcríches, Fearfeasa Ó Maol Chonaire and myself, from
sunrise to sundown, from St Francis's Feast
to Mischief Day, on the list of kings and genealogy
of saints – sifting, straining dates and notes.
On the Feast of Saint Charles of Borromeo, the sisters
baked apples in honour of his blessing of the orchards
and our finishing of the work.

That was the rhythm we took to Donegal and to the *Annals*
– the best days an almost silent meditation, each man
lending weight to the work of the others, light streaming
in the window catching motes or rain dripping
from the leaves all round concentrating the room's sounds
of breath and books. Later – lucubration, redaction
and sometimes a letter from abroad like the one from
Prague on the ghostly library of Strahov we would have
loved to see.

Then the campaign against us, the accusation of the five
errors and that great work still not seeing the light of day.
I carried it with me across the North when the flax fields
were blue to sail from that dark town in July and here
when I smell the retting beds and see the river water
turned to gold, undrinkable – it seems our work is rotting
away too with only my little book of hard words,
an accidental harvest from all the years and journeying.

10

It's words from that book that are lively in my head
tonight and the memory of a marvel. We'd travelled down
to Cloch Uáitéir from Dublin after working on the miracles
of Moling and were staying in the barn of the secular priest
Robneid Purcell to copy his fragment of the life of Kevin
who'd lived with his disciple Solomon on a skerry
in the lough nearby. We copied disgusting poems that day,
I'm ashamed even now to confess.

It was this time of year. I remember the lake
ringed red by the hawthorn hedges and in the evening
we lit a fire on the floor to take the chill off the night,
but as we prayed before sleep the air filled
with the flurry of angels – white wings frantic
and lucent from the flames – our own private Pentecost
overhead in absolution for those godless poems.
Even as we prayed they began to fall, St Francis's flowers.

A flock of great white butterflies bedding down
to winter in the walls had mistaken the heat of our fire
for an early spring and come back to life too soon.
No angels then, but marvellous still. Is that what death
will be, I wonder, a gentle waking into the warmth of
God? These are my last things, my litany of lost
or nearly lost words inflected by home and memories
that flit in the dusk made vivid for a moment, then gone.

I am the poor friar Mícheál Ó Cléirigh.

Acknowledgements

Acknowledgements are due to the editors of the following magazines and periodicals where some of these poems were first published: *Fortnight, The Yellow Nib, Incertus, Poetry Ireland Review, Poems from the Fishhouse, The Honest Ulsterman, Mslexia, FourXFour*.

'The Magdalene Reading' came second in the English Language category of Féile na Filíochta International Poetry Competition in 2000; 'Weather Vane' won first prize in the Strokestown International Poetry Competition in 2007; 'Invoking St Ciaran of Saigher' was written for inclusion in a festschrift for Ciaran Carson, *From the Small Back Room*. In 2008, 'Amelia' was a commission from BBC Northern Ireland for a television documentary to mark the restoration of the Crown Bar in Belfast and was also used in an art installation in the 2014 'University of the Air' Festival to celebrate 50 years of the Open University. 'Disibodenberg' was published in *Die Kirchenlehrerin Hildegard von Bingen* by The Scivias Institute, edited by Dr Antoinette Esser. 'Incunabula' was runner-up in the Mselxia Single Poem Competition in 2013 and was published in Germany in a volume called *Narrenflieger,* edited and translated by Gabrielle Haefs.

An early version of this manuscript was runner-up for the Patrick Kavanagh Prize in 2004 and later versions were Highly Commended in 2015 and 2016.

The author wishes to thank the Ireland Chair of Poetry for a four-week residency at Annaghmakerrig in 2007 as part of the Ireland Chair of Poetry Prize; to all the staff at the Tyrone Guthrie Centre for that and many subsequent visits in which several of these poems were written. Also to

Drumalis Retreat Centre in Larne where work on 'The Winter's Tale' and 'The Work of a Winter' was begun. Thanks also to the Arts Council of Northern Ireland for generous support in three SIAP awards; an Artist Career Enhancement Award and a travel grant which allowed me to attend The Flight of the Earls Conference in St Antony's College, Leuven in 2007 to research the life of Mícheál Ó Cléirigh. Particular thanks to Damian Smyth, Head of Literature and Drama, for his continued support.

Notes

p. 9: Incunabula: the first printed books, a nest, from the Latin for 'cradle', 'cuna'.

p. 22: The reference here is to Othello's injunction as he kills Desdemona. I was studying the play for A Level at the time of the poem's incidents.

p. 29: 'Katherina Knoblauch', a painting by Conrad Faber, is in the National Gallery in Dublin.

p. 31: The story of the Polish Hasidic rabbi who hitches a lift to Palestine on the boat of an Irish queen comes from Abraham J. Heschel's *The Circle of the Baal Shem Tov,* edited by Samuel H. Dresner (University of Chicago Press, 1985). It is only one of three possible legends of how he travelled to Palestine in the 17th century and while the circumstances of the journey are exactly as the Hasidic legend describes, the queen's feelings are entirely my conjecture!

p. 33: Charles of Borromeo was a sixteenth-century Italian cardinal and saint who was said to find public speaking painful due to a stammer and was noted for his compassion to plague victims in his city of Milan.

p. 36: The story told in 'Weather Vane' is my imagined version of exactly this punishment meted out to a young woman in a Catholic convent on the Ormeau Road in Belfast in the 1970s. Subsequently she married and was able to adopt her child. She never told him his birth story.

p. 45: 'The woman of the Rhine' is Hildegard of Bingen and this section of 'The Winter's Tale' owes much to Fiona Maddock's biography, *Hildegard of Bingen: The Woman of Her Age* published in 2001.

p. 48: This poem's title is the title of Jorgen Andersen's exhaustive book on the Sile na Gig – *The Witch in the Wall: Medieval Erotic Sculpture in the British Isles,* and the story on which this is based is recounted by Anderson from archaeologist Edith Guest in the 1930s in County Cork writing in the periodical *Folklore*. I have transposed the events to an earlier period and taken the tale further.

p. 66: 'The Photographer of the Sky' was written after seeing a documentary on Japanese men who retreat to live wild in forests or who go there to commit suicide.

pp 69–70: 'Lilacs from the Field of Mars' and 'Nureyev' owe much to Julie Kavanagh's wonderful biography of Rudolf Nureyev published in 2007.

p. 76: 'The Work of a Winter' attempts to imagine the last thoughts of Franciscan brother Mícheál Ó Cléirigh, one of the authors of *The Annals of the Four Masters*. This is a work of the imagination but I have drawn on, and owe gratitude to, the work of the key contemporary scholars of Ó Cléirigh's life: Bernadette Cunningham, Nollaig Ó Muraíle, Mícheál Mac Craith; Edel Breathnach of the

Mícheál Ó Cléirigh Institute, UCD, and earlier Franciscan scholars, Brian Jennings, Paul Walsh, Felim O'Brien and Canice Mooney. The poem's title, and the book's title, comes from an essay of that name by Paul Walsh published in *The Catholic Bulletin* 28 (1938) and reprinted in *Mícheál Ó Cléirigh: His Associates and St Antony's College, Louvain,* edited by Nollaig Ó Muraile. Paul Walsh used the phrase to describe the work of the particular winter of 1629–30 but I am using it as a description for Ó Cléirigh's life's work. Thanks also to the work of Colman O'Clabaigh, Raymond Gillespie and Salvador Ryan for other historical detail used in the poem. All errors remain my own.

About the Author

photo © Malachi O'Doherty

Maureen Boyle lives in Belfast. She began writing as a child in Sion Mills, County Tyrone, winning a UNESCO medal for a book of poems in 1979 at the age of eighteen. She studied in Trinity College, Dublin and did postgraduate work in the University of East Anglia, the University of Ulster and in 2005 was awarded a Masters in Creative Writing at Queen's University Belfast. She has won various awards including the Ireland Chair of Poetry Prize in 2007 and the Strokestown International Poetry Prize in the same year. In 2013 she won the Fish Short Memoir Prize. She has received support from the Arts Council of Northern Ireland in the form of Individual Arts, ACES and Travel Awards. In 2008 she was commissioned to write a poem on the Crown Bar in Belfast for a BBC documentary, and in 2017 she received the Ireland Chair of Poetry's Inaugural Travel Bursary for work on Anne More, the wife of John Donne. Some of her work has been translated into German. She taught Creative Writing with the Open University for ten years and teaches English in St Dominic's Grammar School in Belfast. *The Work of a Winter* is her debut collection of poetry.